P9-CQV-573

RULERS AND THEIR TIMES

ALEXANDER THE GREAT
and Ancient Greece

by Miriam Greenblatt

BENCHMARK BOOKS

MARSHALL CAVENDISH
NEW YORK

ACKNOWLEDGMENT

With thanks to Sara Phang, doctoral candidate in the
Department of History, Columbia University, New York City,
for her assistance in preparing the manuscript.

Benchmark Books
Marshall Cavendish Corporation
99 White Plains Road
Tarrytown, New York 10591
Copyright © 2000 by Marshall Cavendish Corporation

Library of Congress Cataloging-in-Publication Data
Greenblatt, Miriam.
Alexander the Great and and ancient Greece / by Miriam Greenblatt.
p. cm.—(Rulers and their times)
Includes bibliographical references and index.
Summary: Discusses the rise to power of Alexander the Great, his leadership
and strategic conquests, and everyday life in Greece during his reign.
ISBN 0-7614-0913-0
1. Alexander the Great, 356-323 B.C.—Juvenile literature.2. Greece—Social life
and customs—to 146 B.C.—Juvenile literature. 3. Greece—Civilization—to 146 B.C.—
Sources—Juvenile literature. [1. Alexander, the Great, 356-323 B.C. 2. Greece—Social life
and customs—To 146 B.C.] I. Title. II. Series.
DF234.G686 1999 938′.07′092 [B]—dc21 98-21799 CIP AC

Printed in Hong Kong
3 5 6 4 2

Picture Research by Linda Sykes, Hilton Head, SC
Cover: Musée Archeologique, Istanbul/G.Dagli Orti; pages 7, 46, 49, 51, 57, 62: Erich
Lessing/Louvre/Art Resource; page 9: Erich Lessing/Archaeological Museum, Istanbul/Art Resource;
page 70: Erich Lessing/Archaeological Museum, Naples/Art Resource; page 19: Castel Sant'Angelo,
Rome/Scala/Art Resource; pages 10, 14: Bibliotheque Nationale, Paris; page 5: Roger-Viollet/Bridgeman
Art Library; page 12: Architectural Museum, Istanbul/Bridgeman Art Library; page 32: Musée des
Beaux-Arts, Rouen/Bridgeman Art Library; pages 35, 43: British Museum/Bridgeman Art Library;
page 37: Louvre/Bridgeman Art Library; page 38: National Archaeological Museum,
Athens/Bridgeman Art Library; page 39: Stapleton Collection/Bridgeman Art Library; page 54:
Ashmolean Museum, Oxford/Bridgeman Art Library; page 29: Tom Lovell/National Geographic Image
Sales Collection; page 45: Badisches Landesmuseum, Karlsruhe, Germany/Superstock; page 48: Roman
National Museum/Canali PhotoBank/Superstock; page 56: Silvio Flore/Superstock; page 59: Private
Collection, Milan/Superstock; page 64: Baden Museum, Karlsruhe/Superstock; page 67: National
Gallery, London/Superstock; page 11: Walters Art Gallery, Baltimore, MD

Contents

Conqueror of the World

The kingdom of Macedon lay to the north of Greece. It was a mountainous land that bred tough fighters. Although the people spoke the Greek language, other Greeks looked down on them as uncivilized country cousins. Yet it was a Macedonian king who spread Greek culture throughout much of the known world. His influence was still evident in the first century C.E.,* four hundred years after his death. When Saint Paul and other missionaries preached Christianity, they spoke to people in Greek. When Indian sculptors began making statues of the Buddha, they modeled him after the Greek god Apollo.

The king who accomplished this was Alexander the Great. He did it by conquering an empire of more than one million square miles, larger than any other empire up to that time. And he did it in less than eleven years!

In this book, you will read about how Alexander achieved his victories. You will learn about the way the Greeks of his time lived—the deities they worshipped, the clothes they wore, the

---

*Many systems of dating have been used by different cultures throughout history. This series of books uses B.C.E. (Before Common Era) and C.E. (Common Era) instead of B.C. (Before Christ) and A.D. (Anno Domini) out of respect for the diversity of the world's peoples.

foods they ate, and what they did for entertainment. Finally, you will read some poems, plays, and stories in which the Greeks of ancient times tell us about their feelings and beliefs.

Artists throughout the ages have portrayed Alexander in battle. He was one of the greatest generals the world has ever seen.

PART ONE

Alexander devoted his life and talents largely to warfare. He was noted both for his bravery in battle and for his ability to move his troops swiftly from place to place.

A "Passion for Glory"

Early Years

Alexander was a most determined individual. Nothing could sway him once he had made up his mind. And more often than not, he would make up his mind to do something that others considered impossible.

One such incident was the taming of the horse Bucephalus, which took place when Alexander was around ten years old. Bucephalus, or "ox-head," was a great black stallion that got its name from the ox-shaped mark on its forehead. It was a spirited steed for which Alexander's father, King Philip II of Macedon, was considering paying a small fortune. Bucephalus, however, refused to let anyone mount him, rearing and snorting whenever a groom approached. So at last Philip ordered the horse taken away.

Alexander objected. The problem wasn't the horse, he insisted; it was the grooms, who didn't know how to handle it. But he, Alexander, *did*. When Philip asked his son what penalty he would pay if he were wrong, Alexander replied that he would pay Bucephalus's full price—almost $25,000 in today's money.

Alexander had noticed that Bucephalus was spooked by his own shadow. And the more the horse reared, the longer and more frightening his shadow became. So Alexander turned the steed toward the sun. No sooner did his shadow disappear than Bucephalus grew calm, and Alexander was able to leap onto his back and gallop around the field.

This carving of Alexander riding Bucephalus comes from a sarcophagus, or stone coffin, that was found in the city of Sidon, on the west coast of present-day Turkey. Alexander is racing to help the king of Sidon, whose horse has been attacked by a lion.

"My son," King Philip said, "you will have to find another kingdom. Macedon is too small for you."

Alexander took the words to heart. His kingdom eventually stretched from Greece all the way to India.

Alexander was born in 356 B.C.E. His father spent most of his time trying to extend Macedonian power over the neighboring city-states of Greece. His mother, Olympias, spent most of her time spoiling her son, practicing religious rituals with snakes, and criticizing her husband for his romantic affairs.

Yet despite the quarreling at home, Alexander was brought up to be a good king. A tutor named Leonidas toughened him physically through exercise and a lean diet. He made Alexander march half the night so he would want his breakfast, and then fed him a small breakfast so he would be hungry for dinner. The young prince also learned various military skills: to run swiftly, to ride a horse bareback (neither the saddle nor stirrups had yet been invented), to drive a chariot, and to use a sword and a spear.

Philip, however, knew that a king needed more than physical skills to rule well. He also needed wisdom. So when Alexander turned thirteen, his father hired a new tutor: the Greek philosopher Aristotle. Aristotle was the author or editor of several hundred books and knew so much about so many things that people called him the "master of those who know." He taught Alexander how to

Philip II learned to admire Greek culture during the three years he spent as a hostage in the Greek city-state of Thebes before he became king of Macedon.

think logically. He instilled in the young prince a love for the works of the Greek epic poet Homer, especially the *Iliad*. Written in the eighth century B.C.E., the long poem tells the story of the siege of the walled city of Troy (in present-day Turkey) by the Greeks. Alexander so admired the *Iliad* that he memorized most of its 16,000 or so lines and for the rest of his life slept with a copy of the poem under his pillow. He was also fascinated by what Aristotle taught him about geography, botany, and zoology. In later years, Alexander's army always included scientists who mapped the lands through which they passed and collected hitherto unknown plants and animals for study.

The one area in which Aristotle made no impression whatever on his pupil was political science. The philosopher believed that non-Greeks—*barbaroi*, or "barbarians"—were slaves by nature. He advised the prince to be "a leader to the Greeks and a despot to the barbarians, to look after the former as after friends and relatives, and to deal with the latter as with beasts or plants." Alexander's ideas about government were to take a very different form.

By now, the young prince was a strong, well-built youth bursting

Olympias had good looks and a bad temper. She was very close emotionally to her son.

Physically, Alexander is supposed to have resembled his mother more than his father.

with energy. Like his father, he loved riding and hunting. Although below average in height, he was extremely good-looking. His large eyes were a deep blue, his skin was fair, and his reddish gold hair curled to his shoulders. He was a serious lad—and very ambitious. The story is told that once, after Philip had captured some city, the prince protested, "My father will have everything, and I will have nothing left to conquer!" Like the heroes of the *Iliad*, Alexander had a "passion for glory."

From Soldier to King

When Alexander was sixteen, Aristotle's tutoring ended, and the young prince joined his father's army. By this time, Philip had gained control—through either diplomacy or war—over all the Greek city-states except Athens and Thebes. His goal was to form a united front of Macedonians and Greeks, with himself at its head, and invade the mighty Persian Empire.

The Greeks and the Persians had been enemies for more than two hundred years. Part of the enmity was cultural. The Greeks looked down on people who did not speak Greek. They also felt uncomfortable with the elaborate clothes, perfumes, and furnishings of the Persians. Part of the enmity was intellectual. The Greeks believed they could understand the world around them by means of science. The Persians viewed everything in nature as being directly controlled by the gods, often without rhyme or reason. Part of the enmity was political. The Greeks believed that people had "an inborn right . . . to choose their officials" and that everyone, including a ruler, must obey the law. The Persians, on the other hand, believed in absolute monarchy. Their king, known as the Great King, ruled by divine right and exercised complete control over his subjects.

The military struggle between Greece and Persia had shifted back and forth. Persia completed its conquest of Ionia in 520 B.C.E. (Ionia was an area of Greek colonies along the coast of Asia

Minor, in present-day Turkey. It also included several Greek islands in the Aegean Sea.) Some twenty years later, the Ionian Greeks revolted but were defeated. Persia then invaded mainland Greece to punish the Greeks there for having aided the revolt. But the mainland Greeks succeeded in turning the tables and defeating the Persians. Soon after, they freed Ionia from Persian rule. Several decades later, however, the Persians reconquered Ionia. Now Philip wanted to free Ionia again and avenge the Persian invasion of Greece. He also wanted some of the Persian Empire's tremendous wealth.

First, however, Philip had to defeat Athens and Thebes. The crucial battle took place at Chaeronea in 338 B.C.E. It was Alexander's first taste of combat—and it proved a glorious introduction to war. Mounted on Bucephalus, the prince led the Macedonian cavalry in a thundering charge against the Thebans. In the meantime, Philip and his infantry, or foot soldiers, engaged the

The Great King's palace at Persepolis was made of materials from all parts of the vast Persian Empire. The winged disk above the row of soldiers represents the Persian god Ahura Mazda, or "Lord Wisdom." Unlike the Greeks, the Persians did not picture their gods as people.

Athenians. Philip's army pretended to retreat, then turned and attacked when the Athenian line had thinned. By noon, the Greeks were vanquished. The following year, all the Greek city-states except Sparta formed a federation called the League of Corinth, with Philip as its military commander.

Over the next several months, Philip prepared for his campaign against Persia. But in the summer of 336 B.C.E., before the troops could set sail, he was murdered by one of his bodyguards. Historians disagree about the assassin's motive. Perhaps he was angry over not having been promoted. Perhaps he had been hired by the Persians, or even by Olympias, who was jealous because Philip had married again. In any event, at the age of twenty, Alexander became king of Macedon.

His first task was to solidify his position. Several Greek city-states revolted against Macedonian rule when Philip died. In addition, tribes along Macedon's northern frontier were stirring up trouble. It took the young king two years to subdue all his enemies.

Alexander then began to plan his Persian campaign. His advisers objected. How could his army of only 30,000 infantry and 5,000 cavalry defeat Persian forces said to number 1,000,000? they asked. It was dangerous to leave his kingdom without an heir, they pointed out. But Alexander paid no attention. He was determined to carry out his father's plan, and that was all there was to it. Besides, he really had no choice. Philip's wars had brought Macedon to the verge of bankruptcy, and the only solution was to refill the royal treasury with Persian wealth. Accordingly, Alexander borrowed enough money to supply his troops for one month and in the spring of 334 B.C.E. led his men out of Macedon and east-ward toward Asia. He would never return.

West Against East

Alexander's first actions in Asia were both dramatic and symbolic. As his ship approached the shore, he hurled his javelin into the sandy beach to show that he planned to take the continent by force. Then, as soon as his army had disembarked, he went with a few companions to the ruins of Troy, site of the first Greek invasion of Asia some nine hundred years earlier. There he placed flowers on the supposed grave of the hero Achilles, his legendary Greek ancestor, and ran a ceremonial race around the gravestone. He also picked up several pieces of armor that were said to have remained from the Trojan War and from then on carried the relics with him into battle as good luck charms.

The first battle took place at the Granicus River. The Persian king, Darius III, was so contemptuous of Alexander that he did not bother going to fight in person. He simply sent a force of Persian cavalry and Greek mercenaries (soldiers who fight for money rather than patriotism) to throw the invaders back. The force lined up along the steep east bank of the Granicus, cavalry in front, infantry in back. It was an impressive sight, and Parmenio, Alexander's leading general, advised him to wait until the next day to attack.

Alexander, however, realized that the position of the Persian cavalry meant they could not maneuver easily. Moreover, the bright afternoon sun was shining in their eyes. So he decided to attack at once, before the Persians became aware of their tactical mistake. Sending his infantry directly across the river, he led the main cavalry charge from the right, mounted, as always, on Bucephalus. The struggle was desperate. The river's current swept many Macedonians off their feet even before they reached the opposite bank. A Persian cavalry officer crushed Alexander's plumed helmet with his battle-ax. As another Persian officer raised his sword to stab the king, Alexander's friend Cleitus cut off the attacker's arm with a single blow. The arm fell to the ground with the hand still grasping the sword.

After much savage fighting, the Persian cavalry retreated. Alexander's men did not pursue them, however. Instead, they fell upon the Greek mercenaries and hacked them to pieces for being traitors to the cause of Greek unity. The few mercenaries who survived were shipped back to Macedon as slaves.

Alexander then buried his dead, promised to pay their debts, and exempted their families from future taxes. He also visited every one of his wounded men, made certain they were receiving proper medical attention, and encouraged them "to recount and boast of their exploits." No wonder his troops were utterly devoted to him and followed wherever he led.

Over the next several months, he led them through Ionia, where one city after another welcomed them with open arms. Only the city of Miletus resisted. This gave Alexander another opportunity to show what a first-rate military tactician he was. A Persian fleet of 400 ships carrying some 80,000 men was approaching Miletus to reinforce its garrison. Instead of attacking them, Alexander ordered his fleet simply to blockade Miletus's harbor so the Persian ships could not set their troops ashore. Without the help of the Persian soldiers, Miletus fell before Alexander's army.

Alexander then applied this technique all along the eastern coast of the Aegean Sea. As the cities fell, the Persian fleet also ran into trouble. Without troops on land to collect fresh water and supplies, the fleet—despite its size—could not operate. By the fall of 334 B.C.E., Alexander had captured so many seacoast cities that the mighty Persian fleet was forced to withdraw. It finally surrendered about one and one-half years later.

From Turkey to Egypt

The winter of 333 B.C.E. found Alexander at Gordium, in present-day Turkey. It was in Gordium that he solved the puzzle of the Gordian knot. The tangled knot, which was made of bark, held together the yoke and pole of a two-wheeled wagon that had once belonged to the semilegendary King Midas. It was said that whoever undid the Gordian knot would become ruler of all Asia.

There are two different stories about how Alexander accomplished this feat. According to one, he simply worked the yoke out of the knot. This revealed its ends and made untying it easy. The other story is that he cut the knot with his sword. Both tales fit his personality: he was clever, and he always went right to the point.

The fall of that same year, 333 B.C.E., saw the second major encounter between the Macedonians and the Persians. It took place at Issus, on a narrow coastal plain at the border of present-day Turkey and Syria. This time, Darius III appeared on the battlefield in person. He was an impressive figure: almost six and one-half feet tall at a time when most men stood only about five feet four inches. His silvery hair fell to his shoulders, and his purple cloak of silk gleamed in the sun.

The night after Alexander "cut" the Gordian knot was marked by a severe thunderstorm, a sign that the Greek god Zeus looked with favor on Alexander's invasion of Asia.

For a time, the tide of battle ran in favor of the Persians. Then, once again, Alexander demonstrated his tactical ability. He ordered his infantry to charge despite a heavy shower of arrows from Persian archers. The maneuver so upset Darius that he fled in panic and was followed by most of his men.

Shortly after, Darius sent Alexander a letter. In it, he asked for the return of his mother, wife, and daughters, whom he had abandoned behind the battlefield. In exchange, he offered Alexander an alliance. Alexander replied that if Darius wanted his family back, he should come and ask for them in person. "For the future," Alexander added, "whenever you send to me, send to me as the king of Asia . . . and if you dispute my right to the kingdom, stay and fight another battle for it; but do not run away. For wherever you may be, I intend to march against you." Darius did not respond, and his family became well-treated prisoners of war.

So Alexander marched against Darius. First, however, he took a detour into Egypt. There, as in Ionia, he was welcomed with open arms. (The Egyptians hated the Persians, who had conquered Egypt ten years earlier and had imposed their religion on the people.) There, too, he founded Alexandria, the first and largest of some thirty cities named after himself.

Alexandria, built along the Mediterranean Sea on the western edge of the Nile Delta, soon became a center of commerce and culture. Its population soared to one million people, a heady mixture of not just Greeks and Egyptians but also Persians, Indians, and Jews. As many as 1,200 ships at a time used its docks. The city's museum— the first in the world—conducted scientific experiments and maintained a botanical garden and a zoo. Scholars doing research in the city's library could choose from some 500,000 volumes that had been translated from various foreign languages into Greek. Alexandria would remain a commercial and cultural center for a thousand years. As one historian wrote, its founding was the "most important concrete result of Alexander's life."

While in Egypt, Alexander also visited the shrine of the god Zeus-Ammon at Siwa (in what is now Libya). No one knows what the oracle at the shrine said. But rumors soon arose that the oracle had declared that Alexander was not the son of Philip but the son of a god. From then on, he often wore two rams' horns—the sacred headdress of Ammon—and was known as the Two-Horned One.

Storming Across Persia

Through the spring and summer of 331 B.C.E., Darius and Alexander prepared for their next battle. With his empire at stake, the Persian ruler added new weapons to his arsenal. He had the wheels of his chariots equipped with curved knives that could slash the legs of the enemy's horses and soldiers. He had construction workers smooth out the rough spots on the broad plain of Gaugamela, where he planned to make his stand. Never again would his army be hemmed in the way it had been at Granicus and Issus!

Gaugamela, sometimes called Arbela, turned out to be the decisive battle of the Persian campaign. Once again, Alexander demonstrated his military skills. First, he placed his army at an angle so that the Persian chariots would have to approach over rocky ground instead of a smooth surface. Second, he used his left and right flanks to draw out the Persian line. And third, the minute an opening developed, he sent his best soldiers crashing through the enemy's center. Once again, the Great King galloped away, followed by his men, and the Macedonians were left victorious.

The next few months were almost like a triumphal procession as Alexander moved from one major Persian city to another. At Babylon, the people, happy to be freed from Persian rule, welcomed him with trumpets and showered his army with pink and white flowers. They also turned over their treasury, most of which Alexander distributed among his soldiers. Susa furnished more wealth; Persepolis, still more. In fact, Alexander's share of the loot from Persepolis was reportedly so huge that five hundred camels and four thousand mules were needed to take it to Macedon. After seizing this treasure, Alexander had the royal palace at Persepolis burned to the ground. Some historians claim he was drunk. Most historians, however, point out that Persepolis symbolized the rule of the family of Darius. By destroying the Great King's palace, Alexander showed that *he* was now the leading power in Asia.

Next, Alexander headed north in pursuit of Darius. He caught up with the Great King in the spring of 330 B.C.E., in Ecbatana, just south of the Caspian Sea. But Darius III was dead, stabbed by one of his own men, Bessus. It took Alexander another year to capture the assassin. After cutting off Bessus's nose and ears and having him whipped almost to death, Alexander sent the prisoner back to Ecbatana. There the Persians imposed the traditional punishment for the killing of a king. They bent two saplings to the ground, tied Bessus between them, and then released the saplings. They flew up into the air—and Bessus was ripped apart.

West and East

As Alexander marched across Asia, he became increasingly concerned about how to hold the various parts of his empire together. Unlike his tutor Aristotle and most Greeks, he did not despise *barbaroi*. He believed there were good and bad people in every ethnic and racial group. In his opinion, the only basis for judging people was merit. He wanted to bring West and East closer together.

Alexander began with various administrative acts. He standardized his empire's coinage, so that Greeks and Persians could trade more easily with one another. (Coinage had been invented by the Greeks in Ionia in about 700 B.C.E.) He included Persians as well as Greeks in the governments of provinces and cities. He usually gave administrative power to the Persians, while the Greeks received control over the military and the treasury. He incorporated thousands of Persians and other, smaller ethnic groups into his army and began to train thousands more.

Alexander made cultural as well as administrative changes. He offered sacrifices to the local gods of the areas he conquered. He often wore Persian clothing in public. And he either married or formed a relationship with a Persian woman named Barsine, the widow of one of Darius's generals.

Alexander's changes met with a mixed reception. In general, the Persians were pleased, while the Greeks were unhappy. The Greeks resented the fact that Alexander treated conquered enemies the

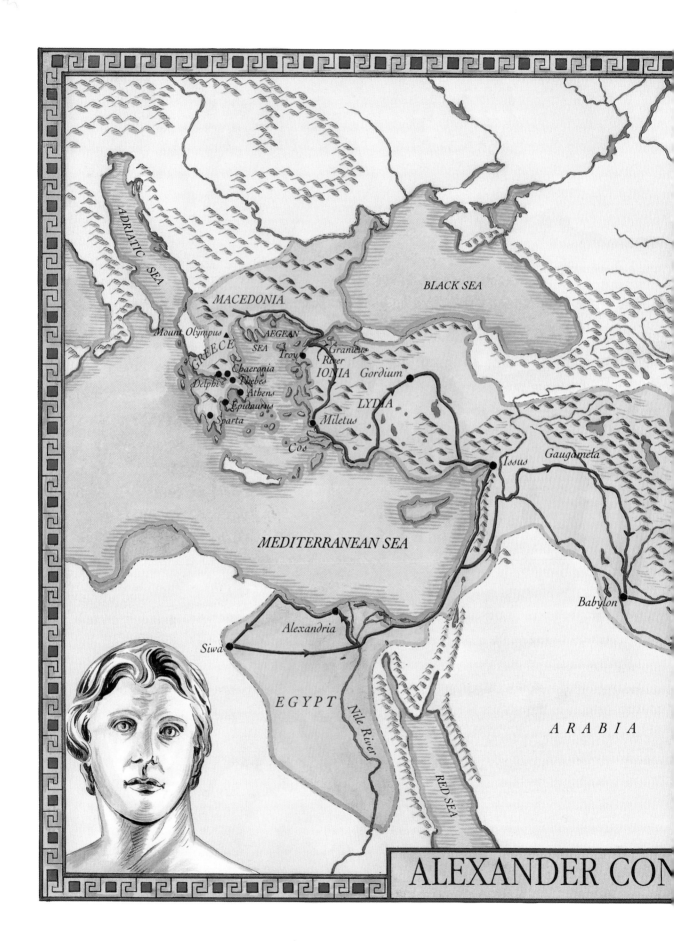

ADRIATIC SEA

MACEDONIA

Mount Olympus

AEGEAN
SEA

GREECE

Chaeronia

Delphi

Thebes

Athens

Epidaurus

Sparta

Troy

Granicus
River

IONIA

Gordium

LYDIA

Miletus

Cos

BLACK SEA

Issus

Gaugamela

MEDITERRANEAN SEA

Babylon

Alexandria

Siwa

EGYPT

Nile River

ARABIA

RED SEA

ALEXANDER CON

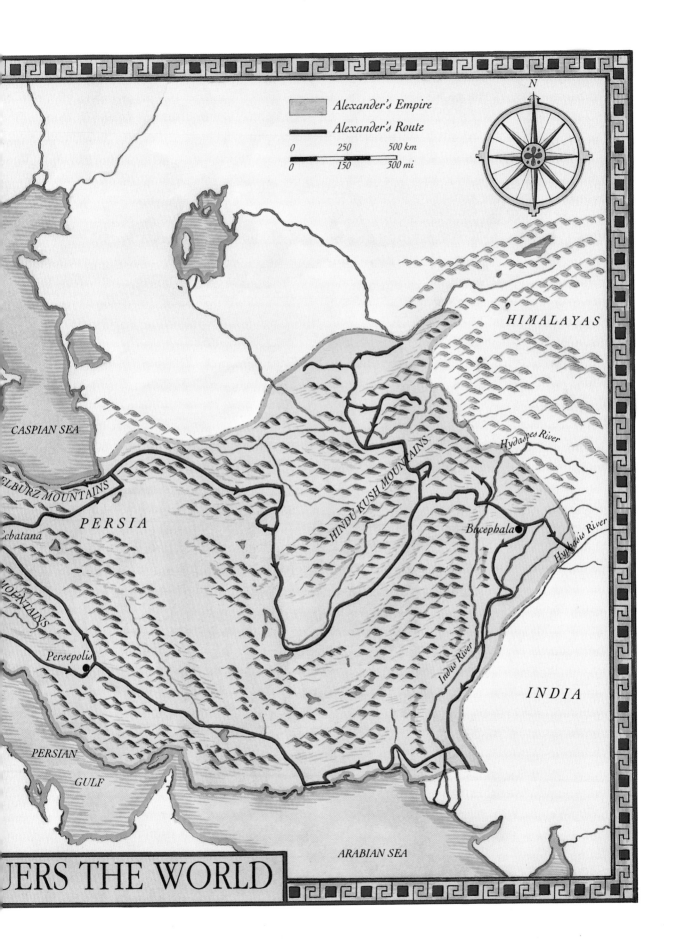

N

CASPIAN SEA

ELBURZ MOUNTAINS

PERSIA

Ecbatana

MOUNTAINS

Persepolis

PERSIAN
GULF

HINDU KUSH MOUNTAINS

HIMALAYAS

Hydaspes River

Bucephala

Hyphasis River

Indus River

INDIA

ARABIAN SEA

Alexander's Empire

Alexander's Route

0   250   500 km

0   150   300 mi

N

UERS THE WORLD

same as loyal Macedonians. They believed that Persian clothes were too fancy and inappropriate for a warrior. They were especially upset when Alexander tried to impose the Persian custom of touching one's forehead to the ground. The Persians considered such an act a mark of respect to a king. But the Macedonians were accustomed to prostrating themselves only before their gods. For them to do so before Alexander meant they were no better than slaves. So they refused. Alexander tried to persuade them to at least bow low before him. But the Macedonians rejected that idea as well, and Alexander finally gave up. By then, though, the incident had damaged his reputation among his troops. Many began to mutter that he was turning into a despot no better than Darius.

Alexander's reputation was even more seriously damaged by his murder of Cleitus, the friend who had saved his life at the battle of Granicus. For some time, Alexander had been drinking heavily to relieve the tensions of warfare and command. One evening in the fall of 328 B.C.E., Alexander and his closest companions, including Cleitus, were at a banquet. Alexander got drunker and drunker. Cleitus then began to rebuke the king, reminding him that he had gotten where he was only at the expense of Macedonian blood. Why was he adopting Persian customs? Cleitus asked. Why was he surrounding himself with flatterers instead of "free-born men who spoke their minds"? Furious at the criticism, Alexander began pelting Cleitus with apples to make him stop. When Cleitus only laughed, Alexander grabbed a spear from a nearby soldier and thrust it into Cleitus's heart.

When he realized what he had done, Alexander was filled with shame and remorse. He tried to drive the spear into his own throat but was prevented from doing so by his bodyguards. He spent the next three days and nights grieving in his tent, neither eating nor drinking. His officers, worried over his behavior, then held a trial, found Cleitus guilty of treason, and decreed that he had deserved to die. But the damage was done. Instead of loving him as they had in the past, from then on many of Alexander's Macedonian troops began to fear him.

The Final Years

In 327 B.C.E., Alexander set off on his last great expedition. He had achieved his goal of defeating the Persian Empire. Now he was determined to conquer the rest of the known world, namely India.

As matters turned out, the Indian campaign was the most difficult of Alexander's career. Part of the reason was that the Greeks had no idea how big India was. They knew nothing about its geography, about the snow-covered ranges of the Hindu Kush and Himalaya Mountains, the sweltering heat and torrential rains of summer, and the millions of deadly snakes that infested the land. They also had a dangerous enemy in King Porus, whose kingdom lay east of the Hydaspes River (a tributary of the Indus River). His army was not only several times larger than Alexander's, but it also included some two hundred trained war elephants whose presence would make it difficult for Alexander to use his cavalry.

The two armies came face-to-face in the summer of 326 B.C.E. And once again, Alexander proved himself a master tactician. He made several false attempts to cross the Hydaspes. Porus at first moved his troops around to meet each attempt. But after a while, he decided that the Macedonians would not really attack until the summer rains were over. So he stopped reacting. That night, Alexander and part of his army secretly crossed the Hydaspes eighteen miles upriver. They managed to draw the Indian cavalry away from the elephants. Then they charged the elephants themselves, shooting arrows at their

After Porus surrendered, he told Alexander that he expected to be treated "like a king." The two men ended up becoming allies, and Porus's kingdom was spared from looting by Alexander's troops.

drivers and throwing javelins at the animals' sensitive trunks. Maddened with pain, the great beasts panicked and began to trample the Indian soldiers around them. At this point, the remaining Macedonians poured across the Hydaspes, and Porus surrendered.

The victory brought Alexander sorrow as well as joy. Bucephalus, the horse he had ridden for almost twenty years, died of wounds and exhaustion. Alexander mourned the death greatly, and founded a city named Bucephala in the horse's honor.

Over the next several months, Alexander led his troops still farther east, to the Hyphasis River (another tributary of the Indus). And there an amazing thing happened. His army went on strike! The men had followed Alexander for eight years and 11,000 miles. Now they would go no farther. As one general put it:

> *With you as our leader we have achieved so many*
> *marvellous successes, but isn't it time now to set some limit?*
> *Surely you can see yourself how few are left of the original*
> *army which began this enterprise. . . . Of all that great army*
> *only a few survive, and even they no longer enjoy the health*
> *they had—while their spirit is simply worn out. One and all*
> *they long to see their parents, if they are still alive, their wives*
> *and children, and their homeland. . . . Sire the sign of a great*
> *man is knowing when to stop.*

So Alexander reluctantly stopped and headed back toward Babylon, which he had made the capital of his empire. But he was curious to know whether there was a sea route between India and Persia. So he decided to follow a different course from the one he had taken on his way east. He divided his army in two. One group of men would sail along the western coast of India. The other group, under his leadership, would travel overland and keep the sailors supplied with fresh food and water.

As matters turned out, the trip back to Persia was a disaster. The coastal area became so rocky that Alexander and his men were forced to move inland and march across a desert. Food was scarce, and the heat was so intense that the army could travel only at night. Thousands of men dropped dead from exhaustion and lack of water. Most of the horses and pack animals likewise died, and the lack of transport meant that sick and injured soldiers had to be left behind. By the time Alexander reached Susa, two months after leaving India, he had lost almost three-fourths of his army.

Over the next two years, Alexander concentrated on setting his empire in order. He put down some local rebellions and either fired or executed government officials who had stolen public money in his absence. He ordered all-weather roads and bridges to be built and wells to be dug in barren areas.

He also tried to bring West and East still closer together by staging a mass wedding. He himself took not just one but two Asian wives, one of them a daughter of Darius III. (He had previously married a Persian princess named Roxane.) He ordered eighty of his top officers to also marry Asian women. And he encouraged the rank and file to follow his example by promising dowries for their brides. Historians estimate that about ten thousand Macedonian-Asian marriages took place.

A different attempt to combine West and East, however, met with strong opposition. Some 30,000 Persian boys had been studying the Greek language and learning Greek methods of fighting. Now they were eighteen years old and ready to join Alexander's army. Accordingly, Alexander announced that he would discharge all his older and injured veterans. Instead of cheering the announcement, however, the Macedonians exploded in anger. What did Alexander mean by dismissing these soldiers and replacing them with barbarians? How dare he treat them in this manner?

Alexander was furious. He reminded his men that they had been nothing but shepherds in Macedon and that now they were conquerors of the world. If they had suffered hardships, so had

Alexander's marriage to the princess Roxane was very popular with his Asian subjects. The couple had one son. Both Roxane and her child were murdered during the armed struggle for power that broke out in Alexander's empire after his death.

he, and he had the wounds to prove it. When would they realize that the Persians were their equals? Then he stormed off and sulked in his tent for two days while the Macedonians begged his forgiveness. Finally, he relented and threw a huge feast in their honor. Nevertheless, ten thousand veterans were forced to retire.

In 323 B.C.E., Alexander set off for Babylon. By the time he reached the capital in April, he was worn out. He had been wounded in the lungs three years earlier. He was drinking even more heavily than before. And he was devastated when his closest childhood friend, Hephaestion, fell ill and died. He still had dreams of glory. He drew up plans for conquering Arabia and leading an expedition around Africa. But his heart was no longer in it.

At the end of May, Alexander came down with stomach cramps and a fever, probably caused by malaria. (Some historians think he may have been poisoned; a few believe he had damaged his liver by excessive drinking.) At first, no one was worried. By the sixth day, however, he developed pneumonia and by the ninth day he was no longer able to speak. His troops filed past his bed to say good-bye to their leader, who waved weakly at those he knew. On June 10, 323 B.C.E., Alexander died.

What had he accomplished during his almost thirty-three years? He was a superb general and one of the greatest conquerors the world has ever seen. He led his army for 22,000 miles without losing a single battle. He was a thoughtful administrator who worked to root out corruption in his government. He did not exploit or enslave the peoples he conquered but tried to improve their well-being through irrigation projects and other public works. He transformed the culture of much of the world. He began the spread of Greek architecture, art, language, and laws around the Mediterranean and into large parts of Asia. He opened the way for Babylonian science and Indian medicine to move westward into Europe. Perhaps most important of all, he fostered the idea that people of different cultures could live together on an equal basis under the same government. Is it any wonder that later generations called him Alexander the Great?

Everyday Life

PART TWO

People in ancient Greece used olive oil as a lamp fuel and also to make soap. It took sixteen years for an olive tree to mature.

in Ancient Greece

Deities, Temples, and Oracles

The culture that Alexander the Great spread throughout much of the known world had reached its height in Greece during the fifth and fourth centuries B.C.E. At that time, Greece was made up of numerous city-states. Each city-state had its own government, armed forces, and money. At the same time, the city-states had certain things in common. One was the Greek language. Another was the routine of daily life. An important part of daily life was the role played by gods and goddesses.

The ancient Greeks believed in hundreds of gods and goddesses. The twelve most important were known as the Olympians because they were thought to live on top of Mount Olympus, the highest mountain in Greece. Each deity presided over a different aspect of life. For example, Aphrodite was the goddess of love and beauty, Ares was the god of war, and Poseidon was the god of earthquakes and the sea.

All Greeks worshipped Zeus, the king of the Olympians and the ruler of the skies. In addition, each city-state adopted a particular deity as its patron. Athens, for example, was protected by Athena, the goddess of wisdom and of arts and crafts, who had given people the olive tree.

The Greeks imagined that their deities looked like physically perfect human beings. They behaved like humans, too—eating, drinking, becoming jealous, quarreling, falling in love, getting married, having children, and playing tricks on one another. At the same time, the deities were all-powerful, and their actions affected the course of human events. The Greeks did not bow down to their gods and goddesses but instead tried to resemble them. All Greeks strove to do the very best they could with the mental and physical gifts the deities had given them.

Greek temples were places where the deities lived rather than sanctuaries where people worshipped. (A Greek worshipping at a temple did so either at the building's threshold or at an altar outside.) The typical temple was built of marble. It was rectangular in

Aphrodite is described in the *Iliad* as being involved in the events that led up to the Trojan War. The Romans later identified her with their goddess Venus.

shape, with an entrance porch at one end. Surrounding the walls stood rows of marble columns. Carvings of both deities and humans filled the space between the tops of the columns and the sloping roof. Inside the temple was a statue of the god or goddess with an altar in front of it. The statue was usually made of marble painted in bright colors, but the Athenian sculptor Phidias made his famous statue of Athena out of ivory and gold on a framework of wood.

The Greeks believed their deities communicated with them at special shrines called oracles. The most famous oracle was the one

Athena was a goddess of war before she became the goddess of wisdom and of arts and crafts. Athenian coins bore her head on one side and her sacred owl on the other side.

The Parthenon, the temple of Athena, is made of marble that contains iron, which causes it to gleam a golden honey in the sun. Its interior was destroyed in 1687 during a war between the Venetians and the Turks when a Venetian shell exploded gunpowder that had been stored inside the temple.

at Delphi. It was dedicated to Apollo, the god of the sun, archery, medicine, music, and truth. Before posing a question to Apollo, the priests determined the god's attitude by sprinkling water on a goat. If the animal stood still, that meant Apollo did not feel like answering the question. If the animal lowered its head or shivered, that meant Apollo was willing to reply. The person asking the question then wrote it down. The priests sacrificed the goat and entered the temple with the question. Inside, a priestess seated on a tripod went into a trance, probably after taking a hallucinogenic drug such as henbane or vervain. The priests recorded her mutterings and interpreted what she—or rather, Apollo speaking through her—had said.

Many of the priestesses' statements had a twofold meaning. The best-known example of this occurred during the sixth century B.C.E. King Croesus of Lydia, who was fighting the Persians, asked what would happen in an upcoming battle. The oracle replied that the king would "destroy a great empire." Croesus thought that meant he would be victorious. As it turned out, the empire that was destroyed was not the Persians' but his!

As years went by, some oracles began to serve as information centers. Many of the petitioners who visited an oracle were foreigners. They brought with them information about trade routes, weather conditions, and good locations for establishing colonies. The priests collected this information and made it available to anyone who wanted it.

The oracles at Epidaurus and on the island of Cos developed into combination hospitals and health resorts. They were temples of Asclepius, the god of medicine. They stood on high, open ground near trees and mineral springs. Their priest-doctors prescribed exercise, a sound diet, proper hygiene, good conversation, and plenty of rest. Greeks from crowded, smelly cities found them excellent places in which to relax.

The most famous priest-doctor of Cos was Hippocrates (about 460–377 B.C.E.), the "father of medicine." He emphasized careful observation and record keeping. He taught that diseases had natural rather than supernatural causes. He placed a great deal of importance on the influence of environment and lifestyle, including the climate, the quality of the soil, a patient's diet, and whether or not a patient was a heavy drinker. He is credited with having drafted the Hippocratic oath, which many doctors today take when they graduate from medical school:

I swear by Apollo . . . to . . . give no deadly medicine to any one if asked. . . . Into whatever houses I enter, I will go into them for the benefit of the sick, and will abstain from every voluntary act of mischief. . . . Whatever . . . I see or hear . . . I will not divulge.

The Great Games

One way the ancient Greeks honored their deities was by holding public festivals. The most famous was the Olympic Games. Dedicated to "the greater glory of Zeus," they were held every four years in midsummer. The Greeks considered the Olympics supremely important. City-states that were at war with one another declared a sacred truce while the Games were going on. The Greek calendar started with the supposed year of the first Olympic Games: 776 B.C.E.

The Olympics included both short and long-distance foot races, a horse race, a chariot race, boxing, wrestling, long jump, discus throw, javelin throw, and the pancratium, a free-for-all fight in which the only tactics barred were biting an opponent and gouging his eyes out. The pancratium was so ferocious, in fact, that it sometimes resulted in death. Nevertheless, the most dangerous event was actually the chariot race. Dozens of four-horse chariots were smashed taking the 180-degree turns on the track.

Except for the charioteers, athletes competed in the nude. Only men could be contestants. Historians disagree as to whether or not single women could watch. But they agree that married women were excluded on pain of death.

Participants in the Olympic Games trained intensively for ten months. Rules were strict. The athletes had to be freeborn Greeks; slaves, foreigners, and convicts could not take part. They had to

Competitors in the chariot race at the Olympic Games cast lots for their position, just like the riders in horse races do today.

register in advance; anyone arriving late was disqualified. They could not use unfair tactics, such as tripping another runner or tampering with someone else's chariot. They could not try to bribe either their opponents or the judges, nor demonstrate against a judge's decision. Anyone breaking a rule was fined.

The Greeks regarded the winners of the games as heroes and crowned them with wreaths of wild olive leaves. Some city-states honored victorious athletes with triumphal parades. Other city-states serenaded them with poems composed for the occasion. Victors also received benefits such as cash gifts, free meals for the rest of their lives, exemption from taxes, and front-row seats at all public festivals.

Going to the Theater

Another religious festival that became supremely important to the Greeks was the one honoring Dionysus, the god of nature and the giver of wine. The celebrations at this festival developed into the world's first plays.

Originally the celebrations consisted of a chorus that chanted and danced stories about Dionysus to the accompaniment of lyre and flute. After a while, the chorus would sometimes fall silent while its leader expressed his thoughts and feelings in a speech. Gradually the speeches grew longer and the choral parts became shorter. Stories about deities other than Dionysus were added, and then stories about the heroes of the Trojan War. Finally, around 500 B.C.E., the poet Aeschylus added a second speaker. Dialogue and action now became possible—and the play was born.

There were two kinds of plays: tragedies and comedies. Tragedies dealt with human suffering and with the way people met the fate the deities had decreed for them. Comedies, which eventually did away with the chorus, poked fun at characters such as the greedy politician, the silly wife, the deceived husband, and the spendthrift son. Comedies always had a happy ending.

Greek theaters were open to the air. The stage was round and level with the ground, while the surrounding semicircle of stone benches climbed the slope of a hill. The theaters held anywhere from 14,000 to 40,000 spectators, who carried cushions on which to sit. Priests of Dionysus occupied the front row of seats, followed by public officials, guests of honor, and ordinary people—including women. Police agents armed with clubs kept order. There was a small admission charge, but the municipal government provided free seats for people who were too poor to pay.

The theaters opened at sunrise. Tragedies were performed in the morning, comedies in the afternoon. At noon, people who were attending for the entire day lunched on cheese, fruit, and wine, which they had brought with them.

An empty wine cup and an actor's mask represent Dionysus's gifts to the Greeks. The worship of Dionysus was especially popular in Macedon.

Men played all the roles. If they were performing a tragedy, they wore thick-soled boots and tall wigs in order to present a larger-than-life appearance. If they were performing a comedy, they padded themselves heavily on the stomach, chest, and legs. All the actors, whether in tragedies or comedies, wore huge canvas-and-plaster masks that were designed to show the characters' age, sex, and whether they were happy or sad. The masks, which fitted completely over the head, had large, funnel-shaped mouths that apparently helped the actors project their voices. Actors portraying deities also carried the deity's particular symbol, such as the bow and arrow for Artemis, goddess of the hunt, or the trident (a three-pointed spear) for Poseidon, god of the sea.

Comedies, like tragedies, were performed only at community festivals. A public official chose the plays and then assigned them to wealthy citizens for staging.

The Greek Family

Except in the city-state of Sparta, Greek families were patriarchal. The father controlled the other family members. He was also responsible for many everyday activities, such as shopping in the marketplace and entertaining friends at dinner parties.

Women were severely restricted. They could not own or manage property. Nor could they vote. In theory, they were not supposed to leave the house except to visit relatives or attend marriages, funerals, and the theater. And even then, they were supposed to be chaperoned by a servant or a slave. In practice, though, poor women held jobs as dressmakers, midwives, and weavers of wool.

Sparta was an exception because it was a militaristic city-state, and Spartan women were expected to produce the strongest soldiers in Greece. Accordingly, Spartan girl babies were fed as well as their brothers (which was not true in other city-states), and young Spartan girls were encouraged to take part in sports. Spartan women had property rights and were not made to stay at home.

The ancient Greeks did not have family names. Instead, they bore a personal name, along with their father's name in the possessive case: for example, Alexander, son of Philip, or Iphigenia, daughter of Agamemnon. Parents frequently chose a name that resembled the name of a god or that indicated the profession they wanted the child to follow. The oldest male child was usually named after his father's father. Girls often received the name of a grandmother.

Women often amused themselves by tossing bone jackstones into the air from the palm of the hand and then catching the stones on the back of the hand.

Marriages were usually arranged by the father, although sometimes a matchmaker was called in to help. In general, women wed when they were fourteen or fifteen, men around thirty. Again, only in Sparta was the custom different. There the marriage age was set at eighteen or nineteen for women and twenty for men. This was supposed to increase a couple's likelihood of bearing healthy children.

On her wedding day, a bride took her dolls and other playthings to a temple of the goddess Artemis (goddess of the hunt and protector of women and children) to show that she was putting away her childhood. After cleansing herself in a river or the sea, she put on a white dress and covered her face with a veil. The bride and groom's families each held separate wedding banquets in their homes. Then the groom and his best man called for the bride at her house and drove her to her new home in a chariot or a cart, surrounded by the wedding party singing religious hymns. When they reached their destination, the groom carried the bride over the threshold while the members of the wedding showered them with fruit and grain so that the deities would give them many children. Inside, the new couple prayed together and shared a light meal in front of a hearth fire. The fire was lit by a torch that the bride's mother had brought from her daughter's former home to her new one.

Weaving cloth at home occupied a considerable amount of a married woman's time. The cloth was woven either plain or patterned.

Living Quarters

The typical Greek house was built of adobe bricks, which were made from earth and straw, then dried in the sun. The bricks were placed on a framework of timber. The sloping roof was thatched with straw and then covered with either hardened mud or terracotta (clay) tiles. The house consisted of several rooms set around an open courtyard that contained an altar and a cistern to catch rainwater. Usually, some chickens and goats could be found there as well. The windows of the rooms faced into the courtyard. The outside walls of the rooms were windowless, for both privacy and protection. Connecting the courtyard with the street was a long, covered entranceway with a door that could be bolted at night.

The main room of the house, where the men ate, was often two stories high and had a columned porch in front. The weaving room, bedrooms, and kitchen occupied the ground floor. The upper floor contained the women's quarters. However, if the family was small or poor, they would rent out the upper floor and install stairs to it that led directly from the street.

At first, the Greeks simply whitewashed the walls inside their houses. By the fourth century B.C.E., however, they were painting murals on the walls or covering them with tapestries. Wealthy Greeks sometimes paneled their walls in bronze, gold, ivory, or elaborately carved wood.

The most important piece of furniture was the couch. The

Greeks used couches not only for sleeping but also for dining, reading, and writing. The couch was made of interlaced leather thongs attached to a wooden frame. A mattress with a soft plush fabric cover was placed on top of the thongs, and several plump cushions enabled people to recline in comfort. The Greeks used small portable tables for eating. Most were round, three-legged, and low enough to be pushed under a couch when not in use.

The Greeks stored their clothes in flat-lidded wooden chests. Many men, however, hung their cloaks on a nail in the wall. They hung other things on nails, too—weapons such as shields and spears, writing tablets, and lyres and similar musical instruments. Wine, oil, grain, fruits, and vegetables were kept in huge clay jars. Reed baskets held the wool for making clothing and tapestries. Indoor lighting came from olive oil lamps made of baked earth or metal. Greeks who ventured out at night carried torches or lanterns made of horn to light their way.

City-dwelling Greeks bought their couches from upholsterers, who also sold coverlets, cushions, and tapestries.

Food and Drink

The staples of the Greek diet were bread made from wheat or barley, goat cheese, and especially fish. Fish dishes included baked turbot, steamed bass, fried shrimp, and smoked herring. The Greeks liked to eat eels and sardines, too. The fish dishes were accompanied by vegetables such as beans, cabbage, lentils, lettuce, and peas. Figs, nuts, and sticky pastries were added on special occasions, as was roasted sheep. Meat was eaten sparingly. Only the Spartans ate meat regularly.

The Greeks flavored their dishes with garlic and onions, used honey as a sweetener, and washed everything down with wine. However, they did not drink the wine at full strength but diluted it with water. Getting drunk was a disgrace!

The typical Greek breakfast consisted only of bread and wine. Lunch was somewhat more substantial, although many Greeks simply ate whatever was left over from the night before. Dinner was the main meal. The Greeks ate everything except soup with their fingers. This was no problem since food was cut into bite-sized pieces in the kitchen before being brought in to eat. Between courses, people wiped their hands on a piece of dough or bread, which they later tossed to the family dog.

Clothes, Cosmetics, and Hairstyles

Greek clothing was usually made of either linen or wool. Only the very rich could afford cotton, muslin, or silk.

Both men and women wore a draped garment called a chiton (KIE-ten) next to the skin. A man's chiton fell in folds to his knees, while a woman's chiton fell in folds to her ankles. One or two belts kept the garment close to the body. At first, chitons were pinned at the shoulder, but after a while they were sewn. Most chitons were either sleeveless or short-sleeved. Long sleeves meant that the person was a slave or a workman.

On top of the chiton, people wore a cloak called a himation (hih-MAY-tee-on). The himation was draped over the left shoulder, under the right arm, and then back over the left shoulder. Men in particular were careful not to drape the himation so short that it was unfashionable or so long that it tripped them up.

Men's clothes were usually bleached white, except in the case of workmen, who dyed their clothes brown or dark gray so they would not show dirt. Women's clothes were usually dyed a bright color, yellow being the most popular. Occasionally a woman would weave a checked or diamond pattern into the fabric.

Both men and women went barefoot indoors. Out-of-doors footwear was either a pair of leather sandals, which were attached

Urban Greeks used a specialist called a fuller to clean their chitons and himations. The fuller rubbed the garments in fuller's earth, a whitish clay, in order to remove stains. People often complained that fullers never returned clothes to their owners on time.

to the foot by straps, or boots made of leather or felt. The most common color was black. Stockings were unknown, but in extremely cold weather, people wrapped their legs in fur or felt.

Women seldom wore hats. They either pulled up their himation or covered their heads with a scarf or a veil. Men went bareheaded in town but in the countryside they wore either skullcaps or shallow hats made of felt.

Women employed a great variety of beauty aids. They whitened their teeth by rubbing them with powdered pumice, a volcanic rock. If their skin was too dark, they lightened it with a cosmetic called ceruse. If their skin was too pale, they patted rouge on their cheeks. Ginger-colored eyebrows were painted black. Short women increased their height by adding a thick layer of cork to their sandals, while tall women wore the thinnest soles they could. Skinny women sewed padding in their chitons to give themselves rounded hips. Women with protruding stomachs padded their bosoms so that their stomachs would seem smaller by comparison.

Until the fourth century B.C.E., most Greek men were longhaired and bearded. When Alexander joined his father's army, he cut his shoulder-length hair at the neck so it would not interfere with his armor. When he became king, he ordered his soldiers to shave their beards in order to prevent the enemy from grabbing them by the chin in close combat. From then on, most Greek men cut their hair short and stopped wearing beards. An exception were the Spartans, who believed that a bushy beard was a sign of manliness.

Women's hairstyles were fairly simple. Many Greek women just let their curls dangle. Others braided their hair on top of their heads or gathered it into a bun at the nape of the neck. They disguised thin spots with partial wigs. Hair ornaments included headbands, long pins, and hairnets. Women also perfumed their hair and often dyed it either blond or jet-black.

Getting an Education

Girls in ancient Greece were educated at home, where their mothers taught them spinning, weaving, and cooking in preparation for marriage. Only rarely did a girl learn how to read and write.

Boys started school when they were seven years old. Except in Sparta, which had public schools that emphasized training for warfare, education was a private affair. Parents paid small fees to schoolteachers and sometimes gave them presents on religious holidays.

Until the age of fourteen, a boy concentrated on letters, numbers, and music. He learned to read by using Homer's two epic poems, the *Iliad* and the *Odyssey*, as his textbooks. He learned to write by scratching a stylus, a pointed wooden instrument, on a wooden tablet coated with wax. It was easy to scrape away a mistake. When the wax was worn down to the wood, a new coat of wax was applied. A boy used pebbles and an abacus, or counting board, to help him learn numbers. Music lessons were given on two instruments, the lyre and the flute.

Most teaching was by imitation and practice. For example, the teacher would recite a poem. Then the class would repeat it after him, either one by one or all together. Similarly, a teacher would play a tune and the pupil would play it after him. Any boy who misbehaved in class was struck with a rod.

Music played a major role in Greek religious festivals, especially those that included dancing, choral singing, and the performance of plays. Here a young man plays the lyre.

The ancient Greeks believed that a sound mind could flourish only in a healthy body. Accordingly, when boys reached fourteen, the curriculum was expanded to include sports. These took place in a gymnasium. It was the custom to exercise naked. The main sport was wrestling. A boy won a bout by forcing both of his opponent's shoulders to the ground three times. After the bout was over, the wrestlers scraped the dirt from their skin with a small metal instrument called a strigil. Then they washed themselves in a tub, and finally rubbed themselves down with olive oil.

In addition to sports, boys between the ages of fourteen and eighteen studied geometry, literature, and rhetoric, or the art of writing and delivering speeches. Some boys also studied astronomy and drawing.

After the fourth century B.C.E., several schools of philosophy arose that provided men over eighteen with the equivalent of a college education. The leading philosopher of the school—someone like Aristotle, for example—would deliver a lecture, or hold a panel discussion with various followers, or pose questions to his listeners. This was considered good training for future lawyers and politicians.

A Day in Town

Greek city dwellers usually woke up at dawn. Their alarm clock was the crowing of roosters, an import from Persia. After washing themselves and eating breakfast, the men headed for the agora, or open marketplace. Although most of them had learned a trade, they preferred to leave as much work as possible in the hands of non-Greeks. What mattered most to Greek men were politics, athletics, and good conversation.

First, however, men did the marketing. The agora was divided into sections. Here stood fishmongers and butchers protecting their products with wicker mats. There were the wine sellers and the flower sellers, shouting to attract customers. Fruit vendors displayed their best olives and figs at the top of their baskets and hid the rotten fruit at the bottom. Merchants weighed produce on a balance scale and put the coins they received inside their cheeks for safekeeping. It was said that a merchant could keep up to twelve coins in his mouth at one time.

Some businesses, such as the upholsterers, were located in special streets leading off the agora. Barbers, shoemakers, money changers, sculptors, and doctors also practiced on special streets. There were areas where men could hire professional cooks, as well as day laborers to work as charioteers, houseboys, and field hands. Horse breeders sold or swapped their animals in one section. The slave market occupied another section.

Surrounding the agora were columned porches where men gathered to exchange gossip and discuss politics and art. The porches protected the men against both the hot rays of the sun and sudden rainstorms. Barbershops were another popular hangout, as were smiths' forges, especially in winter when their fires and stoves provided a welcome warmth.

At noon, activities in the market usually ended. Some men went home for lunch, but the majority bought sausages or honey-covered pancakes from local vendors. Afternoons were spent serving as

Pottery was an important Greek export. The best pots were manufactured in Athenian workshops located in a district called the Kerameikos, from which we get the word *ceramic*. The figures on earlier pots were black; those on later pots were red.

jurors in the law courts that bordered the agora, exercising at a gymnasium, attending a lecture, or going to a public bath. Many of the baths contained gambling rooms, where the men threw dice or played a similar game called knucklebones. In most city-states, the men also participated in meetings of the municipal legislature.

Evenings were frequently devoted to dinner parties for friends (all male). These were often followed by a symposium, a drinking party at which the guests held intellectual discussions while acrobats, girl flutists, and dancers entertained. Sometimes the guests discussed a political or scientific topic, with each man speaking in turn. At other times, they posed riddles to one another. A typical riddle went like this: "When you look at me I also look at you, but without actually seeing you, as I have no eyes; when you talk while looking at me I open my mouth and move my lips, but without talking, as I have no voice." The answer: a mirror. A guest who failed to solve his assigned riddle had to drink a glass of salted wine as a penalty.

The Ways of Battle

Every Greek male served in either the army or the navy. Because Greece was a mountainous country surrounded on three sides by water, most battles were fought at sea—at least until the time of Alexander.

The standard type of warship was the trireme. It was made of wood, measured about 125 feet long and 20 feet wide, and carried a square sail on a forward mast. In addition to the wind, it was powered by three banks of oarsmen, about 170 men in all, who could propel the ship at a top speed of eight to nine miles an hour. The front of the trireme bore a ten-foot-long battering ram made of iron or bronze. A typical naval maneuver was to charge the side of an enemy ship, rip it open with the battering ram, and then hurl spears and arrows at the enemy soldiers as their ship went down.

Greek armies consisted mostly of infantry. Before the fourth century B.C.E., the soldiers—except in Sparta—were amateurs, fighting only when the need arose. (City-states also hired mercenaries from foreign countries.) King Philip II of Macedon, however, created a semiprofessional army whose soldiers trained all year long. They practiced the use of weapons and strengthened themselves by making long marches with heavy packs on their backs.

The typical soldier was called a hoplite. At the time of Alexander, his body armor—which he himself supplied—consisted of bronze

Greek hoplites protected their legs with bronze armor called greaves.

or iron plates sewn onto pieces of leather. On his head he wore a bronze helmet, usually topped with a crest of feathers or horsehair. The helmet extended down to protect his nose and cheeks. A wool cloak provided warmth.

A hoplite's weapons included an iron-tipped spear for long-distance fighting and a two-edged iron sword for hand-to-hand combat. Each hoplite also carried a round bronze shield on his left arm. The shield was large enough to cover the hoplite's body from his neck to his legs.

Hoplites fought in a formation called a phalanx. This consisted of a block of closely packed men several rows deep. Their shields overlapped, with each hoplite's shield protecting the man to his left. Before the fourth century B.C.E., the phalanx was eight rows deep, but Philip II of Macedon doubled the number. He also doubled the length of the hoplites' spears, which made the phalanx look like a giant porcupine from the front.

A phalanx marched straight forward to attack. The hoplites first thrust at the enemy with their spears and then stabbed with their swords. A phalanx was quite powerful. But it was vulnerable on the right flank and had trouble maneuvering.

Because of Greece's mountainous terrain, the cavalry was less important than the infantry. It was also more expensive to belong to, since each cavalryman had to provide and feed his own horse. A Greek army also contained several groups of auxiliary fighters. These were light-armed men who supported the infantry. They were often recruited from outside Greece. The most common auxiliaries were archers and slingers (slingers used slingshots to fling balls made of stone, clay, or lead). Unlike the infantry and cavalry, auxiliaries did not wear armor.

Except for the Spartans, who believed in the superiority of the state, the Greeks valued the individual. Accordingly, up to the time of Alexander, Greeks elected their generals and admirals. A man might be a common soldier in one war and a general in the next war. A hoplite could suggest a plan of action to his commander and have it put to a vote. When Alexander's army went on strike in India, they were in a sense acting within their traditional bounds.

PART THREE

The Greeks

Dances and songs were an important part of Greek culture.

The characters in the *Iliad* display many of the qualities and values the ancient Greeks admired: courage, a desire for glory, devotion to the pursuit of excellence, and respect for the role they believed the gods played in everyday life. In the following excerpt, the Trojan hero Hector issues a challenge to the Greek army:

Hear me—Trojans, Achaeans [Greeks] geared for combat!
I'll speak out what the heart inside me urges.
Our oaths, our sworn truce—Zeus the son of Cronus
throned in the clouds has brought them all to nothing
and all the Father [Zeus] decrees is death for both sides at once.
Until you Argives [Greeks] seize the well-built towers of Troy
or you yourselves are crushed against your ships.
But now,
seeing the best of all Achaeans fill your ranks,
let one whose nerve impels him to fight with me
come striding from your lines, a lone champion
pitted against Prince Hector. Here are the terms
that I set forth—let Zeus look down, my witness!
If that man takes my life with his sharp bronze blade,
he will strip my gear and haul it back to his ships.
But give my body to friends to carry home again,
so Trojan men and Trojan women can do me honor

with fitting rites of fire once I am dead.

But if I kill him and Apollo grants me glory,

I'll strip his gear and haul it back to sacred Troy

and hang it high on the deadly Archer's [Apollo's] temple walls.

But not his body: I'll hand it back to the decked ships,

so the long-haired Achaeans can give him full rites

and heap his barrow [burial mound] high by the broad Hellespont.

And someday one will say, one of the men to come,

steering his oar-swept ship across the wine-dark sea,

"There's the mound of a man who died in the old days,

One of the brave whom glorious Hector killed."

So they will say, someday, and my fame will never die.

According to the *Iliad*, the Greeks succeeded in conquering the Trojans by means of a trick. The Greeks pretended to abandon their siege of Troy but left a wooden horse behind. The Trojans pulled the statue inside their city. Unfortunately for them, the horse was hollow—and Greek soldiers were concealed inside. That night, the Greeks crept out of their hiding place, opened Troy's gates, and let in the rest of their army. Ever since, the term "Trojan horse" has meant an internal enemy.

The sea provided the ancient Greeks with food, salt, and trade routes. Yet some Greeks were more aware of its perils than its benefits. One such Greek was the poet Hesiod, who wrote the following advice around 700 B.C.E.:

If you are afflicted with the desire for uncomfortable travelling over the sea, then remember that the blasts of all the winds rage when the Pleiades [a group of seven stars] . . . set in the misty deep [are below the horizon]. At such a time, keep your boats no longer in the wine-dark sea. . . . Drag up your boat on the land, and pack it tightly around with stones. . . . Put all your fitted tackle in your home. . . . Hang the well-made tiller above the smoke of the fire.

You yourself wait for a journey till the proper season comes. Then pull your swift boat down to the water, and load in it a fitting cargo, that you may bring home profit. . . .

The right season for mortals to sail is fifty days after the solstice, when the burdensome days of summer come to an end. At that time you will not wreck your ship, nor will the sea destroy the men. . . .

Spring is another time for mortals to sail. When the fig-leaf first appears on the branch as big as the mark that a crow makes in the ground, then the sea can be crossed. This is the spring time for sailing. But I do not praise it and it is not pleasant to my heart. . . . It is horrible to die in the waves. I bid you take thought of all these things.

Hesiod gave advice on other topics besides the dangers of sea travel:

> *Invite your friend to dinner; have nothing to do with your enemy.*
> *Invite that man particularly who lives close to you.*
> *If anything, which ought not to happen, happens in your neighborhood, neighbors come as they are to help; relatives dress first.*

The heroes and events of the Trojan War inspired many writers in addition to Homer. Among them was the playwright Euripides, who wrote *The Trojan Women* in 415 B.C.E. While Homer glorified the excitement of battle, Euripides dramatized war's misery and horror. After Troy fell, the Greeks enslaved its women. Among them was Hecuba, mother of the Trojan hero Hector and formerly queen of Troy. Hector's six-year-old son, Astyanax, was also taken prisoner but was later killed. The Greeks dropped the child from the city's walls onto the rocks below. The following speech is delivered by Hecuba over the corpse of Astyanax:

> *You Greeks, your spears are sharp but not your wits.*
> *You feared a child. You murdered him.*
> *Strange murder. You were frightened, then? You thought*
> *he might build up our ruined Troy? And yet*
> *when Hector fought and thousands at his side,*
> *we fell beneath you. Now, when all is lost,*

Parents announced the birth of a son by hanging an olive wreath on the house door. If the baby was a girl, the parents hung a circle of wood.

the city captured and the Trojans dead,
a little child like this made you afraid.
The fear that comes when reason goes away—
Myself, I do not wish to share it.

. . .

Beloved, what a death has come to you.
If you had fallen fighting for the city,
if you had known strong youth and love
and godlike power, if we could think
you had known happiness—if there is
happiness anywhere—
But now . . .

Poor little one. How savagely our ancient walls,
Apollo's towers, have torn away the curls
your mother's fingers wound and where she pressed
her kisses—here where the broken bone grins white—
Oh no—I cannot—
Dear hands, the same dear shape your father's had,
how loosely now you fall. And dear proud lips
forever closed. False words you spoke to me
when you would jump into my bed, call me sweet names
and tell me, Grandmother, when you are dead,
I'll cut off a great lock of hair and lead my soldiers all
to ride out past your tomb.
Not you, but I, old, homeless, childless,
must lay you in your grave, so young,
so miserably dead.
Dear God. How you would run to greet me.
And I would nurse you in my arms, and oh,
so sweet to watch you sleep. All gone.
What could a poet carve upon your tomb?
"A child lies here whom the Greeks feared and slew."
Ah, Greece should boast of that.
Child, they have taken all that was your father's,
but one thing, for your burying, you shall have,
the bronze-barred shield.
It kept safe Hector's mighty arm, but now
it has lost its master.
The grip of his own hand has marked it—dear to me then—
His sweat has stained the rim. . . .
Come, bring such covering for the pitiful dead body
as we still have. God has not left us much
to make a show with. Everything I have

I give you, child.
O men, secure when once good fortune comes—
fools, fools. Fortune's ways—
here now, there now. She springs
away—back—and away, an idiot's dance.
No one is ever always fortunate.

Perhaps the most popular Greek hero was Heracles (later known to the Romans as Hercules). He was said to have been an ancestor of Alexander the Great on his father's side. Heracles' enormous strength is shown in the following story:

Heracles strangles the serpents, to the astonishment of his parents.

One evening, when Heracles had reached the age of eight or ten months or, as others say, one year . . . Alcmene [his mother] having washed . . . her twins [Heracles had a twin brother named Iphicles, who was not heroic at all], laid them to rest under a lamb-fleece coverlet. . . . At midnight, Hera [a goddess who was the wife of Zeus, the god who had supposedly fathered Heracles] sent two prodigious azure-scaled serpents to Amphitryon's [Alcmene's husband] house, with strict orders to destroy Heracles. The gates opened as they approached; they glided through, and over the marble floors to the nursery—their eyes shooting flames, and poison dripping from their fangs.

The twins awoke, to see the serpents writhed above them, with darting, forked tongues. . . . Iphicles screamed, kicked off the coverlet and, in an attempt to escape, rolled . . . to the floor. His frightened cries . . . roused Alcmene. "Up with you, Amphitryon!" she cried. Without waiting to put on his sandals, Amphitryon leaped from the cedar-wood bed, seized his sword which hung close by on the wall, and drew it from its polished sheath. . . . Shouting to his drowsy slaves for lamps and torches, Amphitryon rushed in [to the nursery]; and Heracles, who had not uttered so much as a whimper, proudly displayed the serpents, which he was in the act of strangling, one in either hand. As they died, he laughed, bounced joyfully up and down, and threw them at Amphitryon's feet.

While Alcmene comforted the terror-stricken Iphicles, Amphitryon spread the coverlet over Heracles again, and returned to bed.

Other Greek stories dealt not with heroes but with ordinary people. Many such stories, especially the fables of Aesop, first told in the sixth century B.C.E., try to teach a lesson:

> *A Shepherd-boy beside a stream*
> *"The Wolf, the Wolf," was wont to scream,*
> *And when the Villagers appeared,*
> *He'd laugh and call them silly-eared.*
> *A Wolf at last came down the steep—*
> *"The Wolf, the Wolf—my legs, my sheep!"*
> *The creature had a jolly feast,*
> *Quite undisturbed, on boy and beast.*
>
> *For none believes the liar, forsooth,*
> *Even when the liar speaks the truth.*

One of Aristotle's most influential books is his *Politics*, which he wrote after analyzing the constitutions of 158 city-states:

> *In all states there are three elements; one class is very*
> *rich, another very poor, and a third in a mean. . . . Mod-*
> *eration and the mean are best . . . for in that condition of*
> *life men are most ready to listen to reason. But he who*
> *greatly excels in beauty, strength, birth or wealth, or on*
> *the other hand who is very poor, or very weak, or very*
> *much disgraced, finds it difficult to follow reason. . . .*
> *Those who have too much of the goods of fortune . . . are*
> *neither willing nor able to submit to authority. The evil*
> *begins at home: for when they are boys, by reason of the*
> *luxury in which they are brought up, they never learn . . .*

the habit of obedience. On the other hand, the very poor, who are in the opposite extreme, are too degraded. So that the one class cannot obey, and can only rule despotically; the other knows not how to command and must be ruled like slaves. Thus arises a city, not of freemen, but of masters and slaves, the one despising, the other envying. . . . A city ought to be composed, as far as possible, of equals and similars; and these are generally the middle classes. . . . They do not, like the poor, covet their neighbors' goods; nor do others covet theirs . . . and as they neither plot against others, nor are themselves plotted against, they pass through life safely.

Another Greek philosopher was Diogenes, who lived from about 412 B.C.E. to 323 B.C.E. He was a Cynic, that is, someone who believed in living a simple life and who criticized most human behavior. He knew Alexander the Great. Some historians say he died in Corinth on the very day Alexander died in Babylon. The following stories about Diogenes and Alexander come from a book written in the third century C.E.:

Once when Diogenes was sunning himself . . . Alexander came and stood over him and said, "Ask of me any favor you like." To which he replied, "Stand out of my light."

When some exclaimed about the good fortune of Callisthenes [because he was one of Alexander's close attendants], "Not good," said Diogenes, "but rather ill fortune; for he breakfasts and dines when Alexander thinks fit."

One time Alexander stood opposite him and asked, "Are

you not afraid of me?" "Why, what are you?" said Dio-
genes, "a good thing or a bad?" Alexander answered, "A
good thing." "Who then," said Diogenes, "is afraid of the
good?"

Poets after Alexander's time wrote personal works about individual feelings and experiences. The following poem was written
in the third century B.C.E. by Callimachus to his dead friend and
fellow poet Heraclitus:

They told me, Heraclitus, they told me you were dead,
They brought me bitter news to hear and bitter tears to shed.
I wept as I remembered how often you and I
Had tired the sun with talking and sent him down the sky.

And now that thou art lying, my dear old Carian guest,
A handful of gray ashes, long, long ago at rest,
Still are thy pleasant voices, thy nightingales [Heraclitus's
          poems], awake;
For Death, he taketh all away, but them he cannot take.

Glossary

cavalry: A group of soldiers fighting on horseback.

chaperon: To escort a woman in public to make sure that she behaves properly.

city-state: An independent political unit consisting of a city and the surrounding farmland.

despot: An absolute ruler.

discus: A flat disk for throwing; it was made of either metal or stone.

epic: A long poem that tells of the adventures of heroes in legend or history.

hallucinogenic: Causing visions.

infantry: Soldiers who fight on foot.

javelin: A five-foot-long wooden spear with an iron point; when it struck a shield, the point would bend at the neck, preventing the enemy from pulling the spear out and throwing it back.

oracle: A person through whom a god or goddess was supposed to speak; also, the place where such information was revealed.

pallid: Pale.

philosopher: A person who thinks deeply about life and the world; a lover of wisdom.

political science: The study of government and politics.

solstice: Either the longest day (June 22) or the shortest day (December 22) of the year.

staple: A very important product or crop of a country or region.

tripod: A seat of three legs; a stool.

For Further Reading

Aesop. *Aesop's Fables*. Retold by Anne Galti. San Diego: Harcourt Brace Jovanovich, 1992.

Ash, Maureen. *Alexander the Great*. Chicago: Childrens Press, 1991.

Asimov, Isaac. *The Greeks: A Great Adventure*. Boston: Houghton Mifflin, 1965.

Baker, Rosalie F. and Charles F. III. *Ancient Greeks*. New York: Oxford University Press, 1997.

Connolly, Peter. *The Greek Armies*. Morristown, NJ: Silver Burdett Company, 1979.

Ling, Roger. *The Greek World*. New York: Peter Bedrick Books, 1988.

Mercer, Charles. *Alexander the Great*. New York: American Heritage Publishing Company, 1962.

Nardo, Don. *Life in Ancient Greece*. San Diego: Lucent Books, 1996.

Peach, Susan, and Anne Millard. *The Greeks*. London: Usborne, 1990.

Robinson, Charles Alexander, Jr. *Alexander the Great*. New York: Franklin Watts, 1963.

Schomp, Virginia. *The Ancient Greeks*. New York: Marshall Cavendish, 1996.

Stewart, Gail B. *Alexander the Great*. San Diego: Lucent Books, 1994.

Wepman, Dennis. *Alexander the Great*. New York: Chelsea House Publishers, 1986.

ON-LINE INFORMATION*

http://www.pbs.org/mpt/alexander/resources/main.html/pages
Follow in the footsteps of Alexander the Great. There are good links on this website.

http://www.horus.ics.org.eg/html/alexander_the_great.html
The well-known Alexanderama site, full of information as well as pictures and links.

*Websites change from time to time. For additional on-line information, check with the media specialist at your local library.

Bibliography

Bingham, Marjorie Wall, and Susan Hill Gross. *Women in Ancient Greece and Rome.* St. Louis Park, MN: Glenhurst Publications, 1983.

Bowra, C. M. *Classical Greece.* New York: Time, 1965.

Casson, Lionel. *The Ancient Mariners.* New York: Macmillan, 1964.

Diogenes Laertius. *Lives of the Philosophers.* Chicago: Henry Regnery, 1969.

Fox, Robin Lane. *The Search for Alexander.* Boston: Little, Brown and Company, 1980.

Graves, Robert. *The Greek Myths.* Vol. 2. Baltimore: Penguin Books, 1955.

Green, Peter. *Ancient Greece.* New York: Viking Press, 1973.

Hamilton, Edith. *The Echo of Greece.* New York: W. W. Norton & Company, 1957.

Hammond, N. G. L. *The Genius of Alexander the Great.* Chapel Hill, NC: University of North Carolina Press, 1997.

Knox, Bernard, ed. *The Norton Book of Classical Literature.* New York: Norton, 1993.

Lattimore, Richard, trans. *Hesiod.* Ann Arbor, MI: University of Michigan Press, 1959.

Quennell, Marjorie, and C. H. B. Quennell. *Everyday Things in Ancient Greece.* New York: G. P. Putnam's Sons, 1954.

Robinson, Charles Alexander, Jr. *Alexander the Great.* New York: Franklin Watts, 1963.

Wepman, Dennis. *Alexander the Great.* New York: Chelsea House Publishers, 1986.

Whall, A. L., ed. *The Greek Reader.* Garden City, NY: Doubleday, Doran, 1943.

Winer, Bart. *Life in the Ancient World.* New York: Random House, 1961.

Wood, Michael. *In the Footsteps of Alexander the Great.* Berkeley: U. of CA, 1997.

Notes

Page 9 "My son": Wepman, *Alexander the Great,* p. 14.
Page 11 "a leader to the Greeks": Green, *Ancient Greece,* p. 165.
Page 12 "My father": Wepman, *Alexander the Great,* p. 19.
Page 12 "passion for glory": Hammond, *Alexander the Great,* p. 255.
Page 13 "an inborn right": Hamilton, *The Echo of Greece,* p. 45.
Page 17 "to recount and boast": Stewart, *Alexander the Great,* p. 55.
Page 20 "For the future": Mercer, *Alexander the Great,* p. 78.
Page 21 "most important": Robinson, *Alexander the Great,* p. 65.
Page 26 "free-born men": Stewart, *Alexander the Great,* p. 94.
Page 30 "With you as our leader": Wood, *In the Footsteps of Alexander the Great,* p. 196.
Page 40 "destroy a great empire": Bowra, *Classical Greece,* p. 69.
Page 41 "I swear by Apollo": Bowra, *Classical Greece,* p. 103.
Page 42 "the greater glory": Casson, "The First Olympics," p. 64.
Page 60 "When you look at me": Werner, *Life in Greece in Ancient Times,* p. 73.
Page 66 "Hear me": Homer, *The Iliad,* pp. 216–217.
Page 68 "If you are afflicted": Workman, *They Saw It Happen in Classical Times,* pp. 3–4.
Page 69 "Invite your friend": Lattimore, *Hesiod,* p. 59.
Page 69 "You Greeks": Hamilton, *Three Greek Plays,* pp. 81–83.
Page 73 "One evening": Graves, *The Greek Myths,* p. 91.
Page 74 "A Shepherd-boy": Van Doren, *An Anthology of World Poetry,* p. 327.
Page 74 "In all states": Whall, *The Greek Reader,* p. 765.
Page 75 "Once when Diogenes": Diogenes Laertius, *Lives of the Philosophers,* pp. 137, 140, 148.
Page 76 "They told me, Heraclitus": Knox, *The Norton Book of Classical Literature,* pp. 533–534.

Index

Page numbers for illustrations are in boldface.